Fun Valentine'

for Kids

Valentine's Day is about more than just romantic dinners and decadent chocolate desserts -- it's also about laugher. joy. and being able to smile with loved ones, family, and friends.

This book contains over 100 hilariously sweet & silly Valentine's day jokes for kids that are to crack a smile sweeter than any chocolate.

© Mr. Alae

This book is a work of finction.

Add More Fun!

You can read this joke book with the following rules:

Pick your team, or go one on one.
Sit across from each other & make eye contact.
Take turns reading jokes to each other.

You can make silly faces, funny sound effects etc.

When your opponent laughs,

you get a point! First team to win 3 points, Wins!

What did Ketchup say to the tomatoes?

I love you from my head to-ma-toes.

What did Garlic Bread say to Mint Dip on Valentine's?

You have a pizza of my heart.

What do you call the world's smallest Valentine's Day card?

A valen-teeny.

What did the stamp say to the envelope on Valentine's Day?

I'm stuck on you!

What did one volcano say to the other?

I lava you!

What did the cucumber say to the pickle?

You mean a great dill to me.

Why did the skeleton break up with her boyfriend before Valentine's Day?

Her heart wasn't in it.

What's red on the outside and has you on the inside?

My heart.
Ba-dum-bump!

How did the phone propose to his GF?

He gave her a ring.

What did the paper clip say to the magnet?

I find you very attractive.

How can you save money on Valentine's gifts?

Become single.

What did one Jedi say to the other on Valentine's Day?

Yoda one for me!

What did the one sheep say to the other?

I love ewe!

Why didn't the two dogs make serious Valentine's Day plans?

It was just puppy love.

What did the cook say to his girlfriend?

You're bacon me crazy!

And how did the other sheep respond?

You're not so baaaaaa-d yourself.

What did the couple say after they were struck by Cupid's arrow?

"Ouch!"

HA!! HA!!   HA!! HA!!

What did one light bulb say to the other on Valentine's Day?

I love you watts and watts.

What did the farmer give his wife for Valentine's Day?

Hogs and kisses.

And what did the tweenager give his mom?

Ughs and kisses!

What did one light bulb say to the other light bulb on Valentine's Day?

I wuv you

watts and watts!

What do you say to an octopus on Valentine's Day?

I want to hold your hand, hand, hand, hand, hand, hand, hand, hand!

What do you call a ghost's true love?

Their ghoul-friend.

What do you write in a slug's Valentine's Day card?

Be my Valen-slime!

Knock Knock

Who's there?

Luke

Luke who?

Luke who got a Valentine!

Why is Valentine's Day a good day for a party?

Because you can really party hearty!

What did one mushroom say to the other on Valentine's Day?
"There's so mushroom in my heart for you!"

What do owls say to declare their love?

Owl be yours!

What did one bee say to the other?

I love bee-ing
with you, honey!

Knock Knock

Who's there?
Olive

Olive who?
Olive you!

Why do skunks love Valentine's Day?

They are very scent-imental creatures.

What's the best part about Valentine's Day?

The day after when all the candy is on sale.

What did the painter say to her sweetheart?

I love you with all my art.

What did Robin Hood say to his girlfriend?

Sherwood like to be your valentine.

Why did the sheriff lock up
her boyfriend?

He stole her heart.

HA!! HA!!

HA!! HA!!

What do you call two birds
in love?

Tweethearts!

What shade of red is your heart?

Beat red!

What did one cat say to the other cat on Valentine's Day?

Don't ever change, you're purrrfect.

Why would you want to marry a goalie?

Because he (or she) is a real keeper!

What type of shape is most popular on Valentine's Day?

Acute triangle.

Have you got a date for Valentine's Day?

Yeah, it's February 14th.

What did Frankenstein's monster say to his bride on Valentine's Day?

Be my Valenstein!

What flowers get the most kisses on Valentine's Day?

Tulips (two-lips).

Who always has a date on Valentine's Day?

A calendar.

Knock knock!
Who's there?
Atlas!
Atlas who?
Atlas, it's Valentine's Day!

What kind of candy is never on time?

Choco-LATE.

Why was the rabbit happy?

Because somebunny loved him!

Why don't you ever date a tennis player?

Because love means nothing to them.

What do girl snakes write at the bottom of their letters?

With love and hisses.

What did one squirrel say to the other squirrel on Valentine's Day?

I'm nuts about you!

What did the raspberry say to his valentine?

I love you berry much.

HA!! HA!! HA!! HA!!

What's the most romantic utensil?

A fork because it has Valen-tines.

What Valentine's message
was on the honeycomb?

Bee mine.

What did one oar say to
another?

"Can I interest you
in a little row-mance?"

What are artichokes known for?

Their hearts.

On Valentine's Day, what did the calculator say to the pencil?

"You can count on me".

Did Adam and Eve have a date?

No, they had an Apple.

What did one lovebird say to the other lovebird?

"I love you, TWEET-heart."

What did mama magnet say to daddy iron?

"I find you so attractive."

HA!! HA!!

HA!! HA!!

With whom did Hamburger go on a date?

Meatball

Where did Hamburger and Meatball go on a date?

On the grill!!

HA!! HA!!   HA!! HA!!

What did the shoe say to the lace on Valentine's D ay?

"Please be my SOLE-mate."

How did boy bat and girl bat spend Valentine's Day?

By hanging out together

What did the girl squirrel say to the boy squirrel?

I'm nuts about you!

How did Strawberry propose
Banana?
She said,
"Dear Banana, I love you
berry-much!
Will you marry me?

What did one watermelon
say to the other on
Valentine's Day?
You are
a one-in-a-melon.

Which flower gave the most kisses on Valentine's Day?

TU (two)-LIP

What did a cook say to another on Valentine's Day?

You bake me crazy.

What did the doorbell give to his girlfriend?

A ring

HA!! HA!!   HA!! HA!!

Why do skunks love Valentine's Day?

Because they are so scent-imental!!

What does one bee say to the other on Valentine's Day?

I love you, HONEY!

What did Candle say to Matchstick on Valentine's Day?

You're the perfect MATCH for me!

Why did the cop lock the lady?

Because
she stole his heart

What did one bread slice of a sandwich say to the other?

You are my butter-half.

Name the flower that you don't give to anyone on Valentine's Day.

Cauliflower

Why did the Melon go out with Berries?

Because he couldn't get a date

Pencil met paper and said,

"I had my

"I's" on you

since childhood."

HA!! HA!!   HA!! HA!!

What did the French cat
order at the pastry shop on
Valentine's Day?

Chocolate mousse

Knock Knock!!

Who's there?
It's Pea.
Pea who?
Pea my Valentine!

Name the only vegetable that has a heart.

Artichoke

What did the male whale say to the female whale on Valentine's?

Will you be my WHALE-ntine?

HA!! HA!! HA!! HA!!

Where do bed bugs fall in love?

In the box-spring

What's the most romantic ship?

Court-SHIP

Why did everybody want to be banana's valentine?

Because she is very a-peeling

Vampires always love at first bite!

Why couldn't the mineral water ever get a Valentine?

All of his friendships were so pla-tonic.

What did the romantic sing after she got a paper cut?

I keep bleeding,
keep, keep bleeding love!

When do bed bugs fall in love?

In the spring.

Why is Valentine's Day a good day for a party?

Because you can really party hearty!

HA!! HA!!

HA!! HA!!

Knock Knock.

Who's there?

Bea.

Bea who?

Bea my Valentine!

Why are artichokes so beloved?

They're known
for their hearts.

HA!! HA!!

HA!! HA!!

Which new Taylor Swift tune
is the best couple's song for
two ghosts to share?

Invisible String.

What did the chef give to his wife on Valentine's Day?

A hug and a quiche.

What did one piece of toast say to the other?

"You're my butter half!"

Why is lettuce the most loving vegetable?

Because it's all heart.

Do skunks celebrate Valentine's Day?

Sure, they're very scent-imental!

Knock, knock.

Who's there?

Howard.

Howard who?

Howard you like

to be my Valentine?

What did the boy squirrel say to the girl squirrel on Valentine's Day?

"I'm nuts about you!"

What did the ghost say to his wife on Valentine's Day?

"You look so BOOtiful."

What did the whale say to his sweetheart on Valentine's Day?

"Whale you be mine?"

What do bunnies do when they get married?

Go on a bunnymoon!

What did the chocolate syrup say to the ice cream?

I'm sweet on you.

What did the dustpan say to the broom?

You sweep me off my feet!

What did the tree say to the houseplant?

Do you beleaf in love?